I0615502

Richard Meux Benson

The Magnificat

A Series of Meditations Upon the Song of the Blessed Virgin Mary

Richard Meux Benson

The Magnificat
A Series of Meditations Upon the Song of the Blessed Virgin Mary

ISBN/EAN: 9783744661393

Printed in Europe, USA, Canada, Australia, Japan

Cover: Foto ©Thomas Meinert / pixelio.de

More available books at **www.hansebooks.com**

THE MAGNIFICAT

A Series of Meditations

UPON THE

SONG OF THE BLESSED VIRGIN MARY

BY THE

REV. R. M. BENSON, M.A.

STUDENT OF CHRIST CHURCH
SUPERIOR OF THE MISSION PRIESTS OF S. JOHN THE EVANGELIST
COWLEY

LONDON

J. T. HAYES, 17 HENRIETTA STREET, COVENT GARDEN

1889

CONTENTS.

V.

THE MAJESTY OF THE INCARNATION.

VI.

THE POWER OF GOD.

VII.

THE POWER OF GOD.

VIII.

THE DIVINE HOLINESS.

IX.

THE DISCRIMINATING CHARACTER OF THE DIVINE GOODNESS.

X.

CHRIST THE ARM OF THE LORD.

THE MAGNIFICAT:

A SERIES OF MEDITATIONS.

———◆◇◆———

I.

μεγαλύνει ἡ ψυχή μου τὸν Κύριον.
My soul doth magnify the Lord.

𝕿𝖍𝖊 𝕬𝖈𝖐𝖓𝖔𝖜𝖑𝖊𝖉𝖌𝖒𝖊𝖓𝖙 𝖔𝖋 𝕲𝖔𝖉'𝖘 𝕲𝖗𝖊𝖆𝖙𝖓𝖊𝖘𝖘.

1. That greatness essential.
2. The soul's perception of it.
3. The Divine supremacy.

1. *Magnify.*

a. The creature cannot *give* greatness. It can only *acknowledge* the greatness of God. It is the joy of the creature to give this acknowledgment. By faith we are able to do this now in the power of that grace which faith appropriates. The joy of Heaven shall be to give back this greatness in the full experience of its truth. Our glory shall consist in the utterance of God's glory.

b. God alone is great. To confess His great-

B

ness is to confess the nothingness of all that is outside of Him. We only know His greatness now by considering His exemption from our weakness and littleness. His essential greatness is beyond our understanding. The greatness of the Divine Life in the glory of its Triune activity surpasses our knowledge. But we can confess His freedom from created infirmity.

c. We can only acknowledge this greatness in proportion to our personal experience; and as we only know it by its opposition to created infirmity, we can only acknowledge it in proportion as we know the weakness of the creature. We do not rise to the knowledge of God's greatness by the communication of great powers of apprehension, but by the experience of the great necessities under which we are held captive. Otherwise our idea of God would only be an idol, a monster. But there is no experience of human weakness which has not a correlative knowledge of the greatness of God as its opposite.

2. *My soul.*

a. The perceptive nature of man seeks for God. Material things cannot satisfy it. It cannot be at rest in this lower world. Finite itself, it nevertheless seeks for the infinite.

b. The soul is as it were nothingness developing into infinity. It is formed in God's image and therefore has a capacity of infinity. So a point has the capacity of becoming a line, or rather an infinite number of lines disposed as a circle emanating from it, and thus it expands itself into an infinite pyramid. So the soul expands towards God.

The line is not to be measured by its thickness but by its length: the soul, not by accidents of worldly power, but by the outreaching of faith. That which draws the soul out is love. Faith working by love embraces God. Action towards the creature is soon exhausted, but action towards God—obedience to revelation—what the psalmist calls ' Thy commandment—is exceeding broad.'

c. Personality is the starting point of the soul's action. The impersonal brute has no aim beyond the immediate quieting of the material necessity of the body. Personality is the image of God in the human soul, and seeks that which is beyond all created powers of manifestation, the pure, creative, Personality of God. It cannot be satisfied until it has found that which is like itself, i.e., that in Whose likeness itself was formed.

The individual soul has this longing, and it cannot find rest in any other created individuality, because it is conscious that all such individualities are not self-existent, but point to a kindred origin, the One, the Infinite, the Eternal God.

3. *The Lord.*

a. The Self-existent, the Sovereign, the Covenant God. The soul finds its joy in resting thus upon the Divine supremacy, acknowledging its own inferiority and dependency. We may take the words as equivalent to Jehovah or Adonai. 'The LORD said unto my Lord.' The address may contemplate either the Divine Speaker, or the Incarnate Person. God is Lord to us, our Lord, Adonai, because He is LORD in Himself, the Eternal Jehovah. He does not receive this Lordship from the creature, but abides in the glory thereof, independently of all creation as before creation began.

b. Dependence upon the Self-existent involves obedience to the Self-revealer. We do not acknowledge God's supremacy merely by an act of the understanding, but by the surrender of the will, and therefore of the whole life, to accept Him who has life in Himself as the Master to whom our life must be consecrated. We cannot really perceive God's glory without the entire oblation of our nature to be conformed to His bidding. His infinity makes us sensible of our own nothingness.

c. The Lord must be known not as one of us all, but as the One with whom our soul has the most intimate relationship. All thought of separation is put away in the acknowledgment of union with Him, if He is indeed the Lord, our

Life. His condescension in taking us into covenanted relationship with Himself, does not lead
us to think of any glory of our own as being ours,
but makes us only acknowledge the more fully
that all the glory is only His.

II.

ἠγαλλίασε τὸ πνεῦμά μου ἐπὶ τῷ θεῷ τῷ σωτῆρί μου.

My spirit hath rejoiced in God my Saviour.

The Joy of the Soul in the Life of God.

1. Joyous adoration.
2. Man's spiritual need of Divine joy.
3. The Personal Saviour.

1. *Rejoice.*

a. The joy is the inward reaction of that which is outwardly expressed in magnifying the Lord. The soul does not magnify because it rejoices, but rejoices because it magnifies the Lord. It is the act of magnifying which is the very essence of the joy. We are too apt to contemplate Divine joy as if it could be a vague state of delight, as we may rejoice in the sunshine, or in a work of art or the like; but our joy in the Lord is a joy in the greatness of His Personality which we can only utter by being absorbed into active fellowship with Him. ' Rejoice in the Lord.' The soul would feel itself to be insignificant and miserable if it were not thus taken up in the Divine greatness. As we recognise that greatness we must rejoice.

b. This joy is not associated with any self-con-templative pride.   It is entirely self-forgetful and humble.   We do not rejoice in what we are, but in what He is.   True human joy is in coming out of ourselves.   It follows upon love, by which we lose ourselves in another.   The joy of brutes is that whereby we delight in what our senses receive. Passive delight becomes not man formed in the image of the Creator, formed for action.   Joy belongs to God.   Man cannot rejoice except in proportion as he loses himself and finds God.

c. It is a higher joy to 'rejoice in God my Saviour' than to 'rejoice in the Lord and in His salvation' (1 Sam. ii. 1).   Hannah's was the joy of human exultation, guided by the Holy Ghost, but still needing the Mediatorial Presence to ele-vate it.   Mary's joy was the joy of Divine in-spiration, spoken in substantive union with the Person of the Incarnate Mediator, Who was her joy.

2. *My spirit.*

a. Mary's soul as the principle of human activity magnified God.   The spirit as the prin-ciple of Divine union is the well-spring of the joy. A joy springing out of the human affections is earthly after all.   The spirit is the interior prin-ciple of life wherein God's Spirit comes to dwell, and through which it sanctifies and illuminates both soul and body, both the understanding and the affections. It is therefore the spirit which is the true fountain-head of joy.

b. Abraham *rejoiced* to see the day of Christ. How much more Mary now, with the infant Saviour in her womb. The spirit of man is by nature dead, involving the death of every soul that is born into the world, for the spirit's only life is by the operation of the Holy Ghost, the Spirit of God. That life-giving Spirit operated in a certain degree upon the spirits of devout men before Christ came. He overshadowed them, as now He overshadowed Mary. Yet the spirit raised by a certain influence of Divine life could not act upon the soul or body that was by nature dead, except indeed in a very imperfect manner. Now the Spirit of Christ quickens human nature, not only in His Person, but in the persons of His members. It is not our spirit which, like a harp touched by the wind, utters its melody through our frame. It is the Spirit of Christ like the voice of a sweet singer which vibrates through our frames as being united to His Body, and our spirits quickened thus from within, from Christ's Spirit, through bodily union with Him, rejoice by no mere external influence, but by habitual energy of life.

c. The soul cannot apprehend God, but it lives supernaturally by the energy of the spirit which rejoices in God. The soul deals with the created world as the spirit when quickened deals with the

Creator.   The life of the spirit is of a higher kind
than the life of the soul, consequently the man of
soul [ψυχικός] understandeth not the things of
the Spirit of God.   No amount of natural wisdom
or piety filling the soul elevates it to the apprehension of Divine mysteries.   The spirit alone
can know God with the true energy of Divine
love.   The soul and body of the regenerate are
renovated gradually by the Spirit of Adoption so
as to become through union with the Soul and
Body of Christ the fitting habitation and instru-
ments of the personal spirit—quickened by the
Divine Spirit who proceeds to us in that Body
from the Person of Christ the Head.

3. *God my Saviour.*

a. All mankind, and consequently the Blessed
Virgin Mary, were born in this inheritance of
death, and could only be raised out of it by
the Incarnation of the Divine Person, the
Mediator.   Hence Mary acknowledges Him as
'God my Saviour.'   Purification from the taint of
original sin could not be effected merely by reference to the merits of Christ.   A false idea of
purification by reference to the merits of Christ is
taught on one hand by the maintainers of the
Immaculate Conception, on the other by the
maintainers of the Protestant doctrine of Justifi-
cation.   'Life can be given only *in* the living
Divine nature which man regains *in* a Divine

Mediator—not for Him, nor from Him, but *in* Him. Therefore 'grace and truth' could not precede Christ's coming, but 'came by Him.' He can save none save by taking them up into His own Life.

b. Hannah exulted with a holy but an earthly joy at the deliverance from her state of reproach. Mary rejoiced with a heavenly joy at the presence of Him who is the deliverer of all. She did not receive Divine Life merely because she gave earthly life to Him who was the giver of Divine, but all the earthly affections were by this relationship absorbed in Him who was her Child, and in the form of her Child they laid hold upon God who was thus incarnate. As she ministered to Him of her substance, nourishing Him in the womb, so she could not but receive from Him communications of grace, the return to herself of that filial love in which the Child rejoiced to exert towards her His Divine power.

c. Jesus is *God the Saviour.* His name expresses His worth and office. Mary, perhaps =*bitterness*, now becomes Naomi, pleasantness; or if the name means *rebellion*, now the rebellious race is 'saved by the child-bearing.' The consequences of sin, whether in the heart or in the surroundings, are done away by the Atonement. The fallen race must rejoice in the birth of the Saviour God.

If we would know Him as our Saviour we

must have the same absorbing delight in Him which Mary had. She rejoiced because He came to give the salvation, but He had not then wrought it out. We must much more rejoice because He has now accomplished this great salvation and has made us partakers thereof.

III.

ἐπέβλεψεν ἐπὶ τὴν ταπείνωσιν τῆς δούλης αὐτοῦ.

He hath regarded the low estate of His handmaiden.

The Divine Origin of Salvation.

1. God's watchful Love.
2. Man's state of feebleness.
3. The duty of obedience.

1. *He hath regarded.*

a. Love is the moving power which makes God to be our Saviour. Love is watchful—watchful according to the fulness of power, present to assist, prospective to perfect. Love is discriminating. It recognises individual necessity, helps according to the actual need. It expects a return, namely, that the loved one shall meet its advances with an entire self-surrender. So God looks on man, to obtain for him all the eventual glory of which man's nature is capable, and that glory is the return to God of the love which God has given to man.

b. The regard is not a momentary one. God has been watching throughout—watching for the most convenient moment in which to act,

—what is called in Holy Scripture, 'the fulness of time.'

c. He regards not so as to obviate all difficulty, for that would destroy man's moral position, but so as to order all things with a view to man's moral development by the assistance of grace. His regard gives life. That which He sees lives: that whereon He looks not, perishes.

2. *The low estate.*

a. Man's nature is in a fallen estate. Nothing is low which is true to the order of nature in which God created it, but man was created to live with the power of supernatural righteousness, and he forfeited that by the fall of Adam. Every created thing partakes of the dignity of the Creator to whom it belongs, but man has rebelled against his Creator, and in forfeiting his allegiance forfeits his dignity.

b. Man's nature being thus fallen is liable to all the external evils and indignities which we experience. Other creatures, however insignificant, are satisfied to be what their Creator made them. The worm does not wish to be an elephant. Man is conscious that he ought to have a dignity which he has not got, and therefore he is sensitive to all the necessities which press upon him. He desires what God alone can give—salvation. His true joy is to welcome the Saviour.

c. All the host of glorious intelligences contemplate our low estate. They see us as fallen beings, and have at least some knowledge of what we ought to be. They behold and by God's command they help us in our trouble: but they cannot deliver us out of it. God beholds and delivers. He beholds our low estate by coming to share it, taking upon Himself the likeness of sinful flesh, the experience of the misery in which we, as sinners, are involved. As God He knows what He meant us to be, but God sends His Eternal Son to become man in order to enter along with us into all the sorrows of our ignorance. The Incarnation brings to light the greatness of the Fall.

3. *His handmaiden.*

a. The highest character of man is to be the servant of the Lord. So Moses, Joshua, and David are called. So now Mary. It is a name not of self-will, but of natural truth. Our position in the world is accidental. Our relation to God as His servants is essential. The servant is raised to a further relationship of sonship in the Person of Christ, but man was created to be God's servant antecedently to that elevation.

b. The bondslave has to recognise the absence of any free will on his own part. So must we serve God by nature, simply as God chooses to employ us. A slave has no will of his own, but he knows that he must do his master's will.

Man can have no power of accomplishing his own will, but his wisdom is to recognise his duty towards his Master. The love which must characterise the service of Christians as having been made God's sons must not destroy the sense of necessity which belongs to us as slaves to God in the order of the created world. Even the Son of God from whom our sonship is derived was 'born of a woman, born under the law,' and so takes upon Himself our condition of necessary obedience. His mother acknowledges herself as the bondslave, and so He became, 'taking upon Himself the form of a bondslave.' Nature is not elevated by repudiating its own essential relations, but by accepting the co-operative powers of a higher Life.

c. A slave is not valued by work done but by trustworthiness. We are not to think that we are more truly God's slaves, or more nearly His children, by the possession of any unusual gifts. We must contentedly act within the limits of God's appointment in nature, learning obedience by the things which we suffer, that so we may be able to use the freedom of God's children in the accomplishment of all those purposes which He by grace will teach us to desire and strengthen us to do. Our necessary obedience, as slaves by nature, must prepare for the voluntary glorification which as sons we are to give to God by grace.

IV.

ἀπὸ τοῦ νῦν μακαριοῦσί με πᾶσαι αἱ γενεαί.

From henceforth all generations shall count me happy.

𝕿𝖍𝖊 𝕴𝖓𝖈𝖆𝖗𝖓𝖆𝖙𝖎𝖔𝖓 𝖙𝖍𝖊 𝕭𝖊𝖌𝖎𝖓𝖓𝖎𝖓𝖌 𝖔𝖋 𝕿𝖗𝖚𝖊 𝕵𝖔𝖞 𝖋𝖔𝖗 𝕸𝖆𝖓.

1. Christ the giver of joy.
2. The joy of humanity in union with Him.
3. The perpetuity of that joy.

1. *From henceforth.*

a. The Incarnation is the beginning of all blessings. The Word of God is Himself in every way 'the Beginning' [αὐτὸς πρωτεύων]; Himself the first. So the years of grace are dated from His birth. It was the turning point of the history of the human race, the advent of the second Adam.

b. Up to that time man's nature was empty. Preventing grace there was, the overshadowing of the Holy Ghost, but not indwelling grace. Mary was κεχαριτωμένη, prepared by grace to receive the Divine Person who should be born of her. Jesus was 'full of grace and truth,' having the grace inherent in the temple of His Body.　The law had empty shadows of good things to come, but the image of the things is substantially communicated to us in the ordinances of the Church, the Body of Christ.

c. The Person of the Son of God came in all His fulness to be the Child of Mary as man.　From the first moment of her pregnancy He claimed as His own the Body that was formed within her, taken from her substance.　The blessedness of the maternity was complete before the maturity of the humanity.

2. *Account me happy.*

a. The woman was to be ' saved through the child-bearing.'　That which was given to woman as her penalty was intended to be eventually her joy.　That joy Mary now receives, a joy to be eventually perfected in the final manifestation of the Body of Christ, when all the saints shall enter into the joy of their Lord.

b. Mary probably speaks here not so much of her personal joy as of the joy of humanity.　Mary is the representative of humanity, the woman who was the especial object of the serpent's hatred. Humanity, although the parent of a heavenly seed, has been cast down for a time to earth to suffer much affliction from the dragon, but shall appear at last, triumphant over every difficulty, as the City of God, the Bride of Christ.

C

c. The Church calls Mary happy, by sharing that happiness and exulting in union with Christ. The joy of the elect humanity which began in the bitterness of our state of humiliation in the form of maternity shall be consummated in the glory of the state of exaltation in the form of bridal, the Marriage Supper of the Lamb. 'As a young man marrieth a virgin, so shall thy sons marry thee, and as the bridegroom rejoiceth over the bride, so shall thy God rejoice over thee.' As Eve was both the daughter and the bride of Adam, so is humanity both the mother and the bride of the second Adam. Her sons include those who are taken into the glorified humanity of Christ the Firstborn, partakers in Him of the Divine Life and the Divine joy. The suffering joy of the maternity which has a sword piercing the heart, by reason of this very union, is changed into the perfect joy of indissoluble union in the bliss of God.

d. The only other place where the word 'account happy' occurs is in St. James, 'Behold we count them happy which endure.' The beginning of all happiness is the Incarnation. The only happiness in this world is to share Christ's cross and to suffer. 'If ye suffer with Christ happy are ye.' The true, the final happiness is in the manifestation of the kingdom of Heaven, the glory of the Heavenly Jerusalem. 'Happy are they which are called to the Marriage Supper of the Lamb.'

3. *All generations.*

a. The grace which came by Christ was not
to be an evanescent manifestation, it was to abide
from generation to generation. As Mary now,
so, but in a yet higher way, would all future
generations be taken into union with the Incarnate
Lord after His Ascension. Only they who are
taken into this union can know her joy in her
Saviour.

b. The Son of God took her substance and
separated it by Divine Life from her person, that
He might act therein in the perfection of His Godhead. In the Christian Church He takes our
persons, separating us from the corrupt substance
of our humanity, that as we are partakers of His
glorified Humanity and of His glorifying Godhead,
He may act beneath the evil of our outward
humanity which has to be done away, and may
make us to be identified with Himself by grace,
in the perfection of the Divine Righteousness.
' Happy is she that believed, for there shall be an
accomplishment of those things which were told
her of the Lord.' ' Happy in all ages they who
hear the word of God and keep it ' (Luke xi. 28).
' Happy if they be reproached for the name of
Christ, for the Spirit of glory and of God resteth
upon them ' (1 Peter iv. 14). ' Happy the dead
who die in the Lord ' (Rev. xiv. 13). ' Happy and
holy is he that hath part in the first resurrection ;

on such the second death hath no power' (Rev.
xx. 8). 'Happy they that do His commandments,
that they may have right to the tree of life, and
may enter in through the gates into the city.'

c. The joy of the Incarnation is the strength
of each successive generation in its suffering. The
joy of the Incarnation shall be the united consciousness of all generations when they shall be
gathered together singing Alleluia. Then shall
the elect humanity indeed be manifest as the
Naomi, full of pleasantness and delight, no longer
widowed, but rejoicing in the bridal of eternity.

V.

ἐποίησέ μοι μεγαλεῖα ὁ δυνατός.

He that is mighty hath done to me great things.

The Majesty of the Incarnation.

1. The fulfilment of Divine promises.
2. The work of the Incarnation surpassing the
   work of Creation.
. 3. The infinite glory of man's destiny.

1. *Hath done to me.*

a. The action of God is beginning now to develop the promises of God.   God manifests Himself by His Word, but His Word is an active word,
and therefore can only be fully known by that
which it accomplishes.

b. That which God does is something which
really affects ourselves.   God's gifts are not
merely external.   He does not merely give something to us, He does something for us.   Such
action of God implies a real change in the recipient.   So the Blessed Virgin hereby became the
Mother of God.   This was the elevation of nature
into a new relationship to God.   The creature

could not rise to such elevation by any effort.   It
was a vocation—a call of the Creator, a manifestation of the Word, by whom all things are created,
calling her to this relationship by the action
of the Holy Ghost upon her physical frame.   So
by the action of God's grace upon us our nature
becomes pregnant as it were with Divine powers
according to the manner of the Divine call.   The
action of the Creator towards us is of necessity a transformation whereby our very nature is
elevated.

c. God's action is a continuous action, not a
solitary or transitory one.   This is expressed by
the aorist.   The happiness of which Mary speaks
is the outcome of a continuous activity of God.
So must we recognise the continuous Personal
action of God towards us, sustaining us in that
life of grace to which He calls us.

2. *Great things.*

a. The wonderful works of God are the manifestation of God in the flesh by the Incarnation and
the extension of that Incarnation in the Church.
The only other place where the word occurs is
upon the day of Pentecost.   All created things
are small to the Creator.   Nothing He does can
be great unless His action enshrines Himself.   He
alone is great: He alone the greatness of any of
His works.

b. The greatness which is in God obtains a

manifoldness by manifestation in created form. Every feature of created littleness becomes expanded by the corresponding greatness of Divine glory. Indeed, the greatness of the undivided glory of God shining upon the creature reveals the manifold littleness of the creature as it pours into that littleness the quickening greatness of the Divine Life.

c. The great things which God does for us, do not affect the littleness which belongs to us in the order of nature so as to make us in any way superior to the exigencies of natural position. Nature remains nature in all its feebleness although filled with the majesty of heavenly glory in the fellowship of Divine action.

3. *He that is mighty.*

a. It is a greater act of power whereby God takes the creature into union with Himself than it was when He called the creature out of nothing. The Eternal Power and Godhead of the Creator are seen by the things which are made, but the things made are themselves evanescent. The act of the Divine Power is eternal. His power is not merely a supreme mechanical power, but a living Personal power.

b. The Father is Almighty; so is the Son; so is the Holy Ghost: and yet they are not three Almighties but one Almighty. The Almighty Love of the Father is the moving principle of the

Incarnation. God sent His Son. The Action of the Godhead contains within itself the eternal relationships of the Three Divine Persons. This unity is the very basis of the Divine Life. The Almighty is the Everlasting.

c. The living Unity of the Three Divine Persons is the Eternal Love, and the outcome of the Divine Power assuming the creature into any participation of its greatness is the communication of the Divine Love to the creature. God is Love, and there can be no essential action of the Divine Power which is not the action of Divine Love. Nothing could be truly the great work of the Almighty which was not the communication of the Eternal Love. As we contemplate the Divine Love thus acting towards man by the Incarnation, we must remember that we cannot live in the power of that which God has done unless we live in the reciprocal action of love to which we are called by this supernatural exaltation. Our personal action is not destroyed by the greatness of what God does for us, but we must rise in personal response to the greatness of that love whereby He who calls us empowers us. Our love to God is no merely human affection however great, but it is an exercise of the Divine Power, raising us above nature so that we act in the fellowship of God.

VI.

ὁ δυνατός.

He that is mighty.

The Power of God.

1. Personal.
2. Self-originative.
3. Creative.

1. *God's power is personal.*

a. He does not merely possess power as an acquisition, but as a property inherent in His Personality. The person of any man is weak, however great may be the power that he possesses. He can lose it. He is dependent upon various contingencies for its exercise. God has all power, not residing in Himself but originating in Himself. He is not dependent upon any external conditions for the use of His power. He lives eternally by the eternal power inherent in Himself.

b. His power is none the less nor any the more because it is exerted towards beings outside of Himself. His power is formulated by His own Will. The eternal action of His power within Himself is shown in the eternal generation of the Son and the Eternal Procession of the Holy Ghost.

c. He is Himself the sphere within which His infinite power acts, and without the eternal interior activity on which the Divine relationships are based, His power would have no adequate sphere of action, nor result of effort. There can be no adequate result of Divine power which is not itself truly Divine. If the Divine Persons were not consubstantial with the Father, the Divine Almightiness would waste itself in coming outside of the Divine Substance.

2. *God's personal power is self-originative.*

a. He does not act under the stress of any external necessity. His eternal volition is the eternal cause of His interior action. Without this He would be a dead unconscious immensity. His eternal will changes not. By this will He lives. Life is action. His action must be within Himself. His action must be equal with Himself. The Son, the Spirit must be consubstantial, co-equal with the Father, co-eternal with the Father's changeless will.

b. The Divine Person generated thus within the Godhead must be the true Image of the Father; for if He were in any way inferior to the Father, the action of the Godhead would have been untrue. The result must be identical with the origin.

There can be no Third Person thus generated within the Substance of the Godhead; for if the act of generation were repeated, each act would be but a partial act, lacking the completeness of Divine Life.

c. The Second Person being the Image of the First must be, like the First, an originative Person. He does not indeed originate another Person from Himself as He Himself is originated from the Father. If He did so, He would come between the First and the Third Person, and there would be an interruption of the energy of the Divine Power by the transmission through successive generations. He is the perfect Image of the Father, and He originates the Third Person as the Father does. It is not an imitative act, but it is an act of identity. ' He and the Father are one ' in Life, and therefore the Life common to both originates the Third Person by the procession of living Power from both, one and the same Power because they live in one and the same Almighty Substance.

d. If the Holy Ghost proceeding from them both were not a person, the living Substance of the Godhead would have lost one of its characteristics. The Act of the Procession would be unequal to the glory of the Father and the Son. But that cannot be. Therefore the Third Person of the Godhead is the manifestation of unity of Life unbroken, wherein the Father and the Son dwell eternally, and the Godhead thus proceeding remains personal in its Life, and this Third Person is of one substance, power, and eternity with the Father and the Son.

e. In the Procession of the Holy Ghost the act of the Divine Substance finds a term. Without that Procession the Divine Substance would have been broken in two by the generation of the Second Person. But the exercise of the Divine Substance by the two in the undivided act of Procession precludes any such division. The Substance of the Godhead proceeds in the Unity of the Person of the Holy Ghost.

The Monarchy of the Father and the Procession of the Holy Ghost are the bond of the Eternal Trinity.

f. The eternal act of the Divine Substance does not tolerate repetition so that there should be an infinite number of Trinities springing up after the manner of the primary Trinity. The action of the Divine Substance is eternal, not consecutive. The action of the Holy Ghost is a Divine reflex action of love towards the Father and the Son from whom He proceeds.

3. *The creative power.*

a. The exhaustless power of the Godhead finds a new form of action in the Person of the Holy Ghost proceeding so as to accomplish works outside of God, but not the less worthy of God.

b. The act of the Holy Ghost is incapable of

repetition, but the power of the Godhead remains unimpaired. The Holy Ghost proceeds *ad extra*.

This creative action has a numerical infinity commensurate with its eternal origin. Otherwise it would not be worthy of God. But it loses the Personal Infinity of the Godhead, for it goes forth to act outside of the Divine Nature.

c. There can be no Divine Person outside of the Divine Substance. Creation has no substantial necessity, being outside of the Eternal Life, but it is the act of the Divine volition of the Three Almighty Persons. For the same reason it lacks permanence, but in its constant flux it mirrors the eternal purposes of the Divine goodness which the all-originating volition is pleased to stamp upon its nothingness.

VII.

ὁ δυνατός.

He that is mighty.

The Power of God.

1. Universal.
2. Voluntary.
3. Beneficent.

1. *God's power is universal.*

a. He is not more powerful than others, but He is the only being who has any power, and the power of all others is only by communication from Him. He cannot even *give* them power, but all the power which they exercise, whether material or intellectual, individual or collective, is only by His continued and unchanging presence sustaining them each and all, both good and bad.

b. Even the power of thought is communicated from Him and exercised in Him, so that it is impossible for any human or angelic being to conceive of that which is beyond His power. All our thoughts come short of His mind. We cannot conceive a better world or anything better in the world than what He has purposed and will perform. To conceive of anything which He has not taught us to conceive would be a creative act, and He is the only Creator. We may conceive of impossible combinations, but the things which our mind combines are His creation, and the combinations which are not His will would be injurious developments, not augmenting power but effacing it.

So then not only all actual power but all possible power comes from Him. He is not comprehended within any limits which hinder His power, nor surrounded by any vacancy in which His power ceases to act. On the contrary, all created things are contained in Him, so that it is impossible for the created mind to wander beyond the outlines of His predestination. We may rebel against what He has ordained, but we cannot form to ourselves any object of contemplation except according to the laws which He has given. Any such combinations are only like the grotesque monsters of ancient sculpture.

c. Hence the power of God is as truly *one* as it is universal. This we find scientifically enforced by the laws of comparative anatomy and the like. However great the variety of things may be, all things bear the impress of the same origin. This origin is a living and a life-giving origin. Whatever, therefore, is not in accordance with the original law thus impressed, must be a deformity, a thing of death. Created life can only be in accordance with the impressed law of the uncreated life.

2. *God's power is voluntary.*

a. God does not live subject to any power, but He is the Author of all power. It is engendered from Him. The created world follows upon the eternal activity of God, because God creates all things by His only-begotten Son. If it were not for the interior act of the eternal generation of His Son, and the procession of the Holy Ghost in the act of this eternal generation, the created world must be one with the unintelligent First Cause, which without any will of His own gave existence to all. All must be one with God, or else all must be nothing. The mediation of the Word is as essential to the primary creation of the world as it is to the world's restoration, and the new creation in holiness.

b. All that *is to be* has been present to the mind of God from eternity in His only-begotten Son. All that *could be for good* is to be, and has thus been present to the mind of God and will eventually be. If there were any good which will be wanting to the final development of creation, then something would be wanting to the Divine goodness. God would be imperfect. He is perfect in Himself, and He is putting forth His perfections by creative power. All that power is exercised through His consubstantial Son. His Spirit proceeding holds that which He creates in union with Himself and in conformity to His will.

c. The will of God does not spring from necessity, but necessity springs from His will. If we rebel against His will or seek something which His will has not ordained, we set ourselves not merely against facts, so as to fail, but against the Creator, so as to fail eternally. The eternal failure is not a mere failure to accomplish what we seek, a disappointment, but it is an antagonism to the eternal will which alone can give happiness, and therefore it is an eternal penalty. Nothing passes out of existence because it does not choose to submit to the eternal sovereign will. That will must triumph. The rebellious must experience throughout eternity the antagonism of the Divine Omnipotence. The will of God accomplishes by its own unexhausted energy in some new form of creation that which the rebellious creature has refused to carry into effect.

3. *God's power is beneficent.*

a. The will of the All-good is altogether good. Whatever He originates is good, and whatever is good is sure to be originated by Him. It is not in God's power to originate anything that is not good, for whatever is not good is destructive of something which is good. Nothing is simply bad in itself, but only by relation to other things. It is bad because it is antagonistic to something which is good.   But the power of God cannot be self-destructive.   If He destroyed anything that He had made, He would be 'denying Himself,' as St. Paul says.

b. His goodness is a living power in all those who embrace it, so that it is continually developing itself in consequences of beneficence.   God's acts are not merely things good for a time and perishing, but good for ever, in ever-fresh germination of enjoyment.

c. The punishment of the rebellious is God's strange work, not His own work but their own work upon themselves.   He created that which is evil, but He created it to be good.   The purpose of His beneficence is not frustrated because He creates others to enjoy what has been thus thrown away, but His anger is not malicious revenge.   It is changeless love which becomes the destruction of those who reject it, because they reject that which love provided for their good, and it now goes on acting with necessary destructiveness against everything that is opposed.   The rebellious creature does not regain the co-operation of God's beneficent will by mere self-surrender after conflicts. The past antagonism to God's will remains and needs to be obliterated.   Otherwise there can be no reconciliation.   God's beneficent will has been acting all along, and there has been a heaping up of wrath by those who resisted it. This needs to be done away.   Otherwise there can be no atonement. When we say that God must be reconciled to us, we are stating an historical fact. It is not that God's will must be changed. That has been, is, and ever will be, ceaseless love, but man cannot ask to be accepted of God as if starting anew. There must be a Divine act for the doing away of the past offences before there can be a rightful co-operation for the future. God's beneficence requires us to become worthy and co-operative partakers of His goodness, and not merely to accept His goodness by compulsion.

VIII.

ἅγιον τὸ ὄνομα αὐτοῦ.

Holy is His Name.

The Divine Holiness.

1. The Divine nature essentially holy.
2. The Divine covenant sanctifying.
3. The consciousness of God's holiness in the children of His covenant.

1. *The Holiness of God.*

a. The beneficence of God is not a mere attention to the well-being or external happiness of His creatures. His power is a moral power. His beneficence is true beneficence, effecting the sanctification of those who accept it. He is holy, and He makes holy. His power is not a mere neutral capacity, such as is the power residing in any created being. Power may be used by us well or ill. Not so the power of God. His power ever active is also always holy. A creature possessing power is always liable to misuse that power. God is never mastered by the power which He exerts, for He originates that power from Himself. He always knows how to use it. He develops power according to the will of His infinite Wisdom, and uses it for the purpose of infinite Love. We seek by power to escape from God's control, and so we fall into sin. He develops His own will by the external results of His power, and exercises His holy sovereignty. His power is never mere brute force or mechanical supremacy. His power is always the operation of love for the glory of His dear Son.

b. A being is holy whose action results in the well-being of everything. Holiness promotes the relative well-being, while it promotes individual well-being. That which has within it any element of destruction would not be holy, but God is so preservative that He eliminates everything that would destroy. He destroys the power of evil. Stagnation or cessation of power is evil. God so preserves that which springs from Him that He makes it to be perpetually effective for good.

The holiness of God is therefore a beneficent life-generating energy. It is not merely free from taint of evil. It is radiant with elements of good, which it communicates to all who are capable of accepting the good, so as to accomplish His designs of goodness.

c. The holiness of each Person of the Eternal Trinity is the eternal action of this power as originating, originated, and continuously unexhausted. The thrice-holy God communicates His own holiness to the creature, which in itself can have no holiness, for it has within itself no inherent life.

This holiness is communicated by the assumption of our humanity into union with one of the Divine Persons. No human person is capable of possessing this holiness. The Person of the Son of God assuming our nature into union with Himself makes it to be the instrument of the Divine holiness, and all other beings are capable of being made holy only by being taken up into union with the nature thus assumed.

2. *His Name.*

a. The Psalmist had sung, ' Let them praise Thy Name, for it is great, fearful, and holy.' The holiness for which He is to be magnified is inherent in His Name. It is no mere possession which may be alienated. It is derived from His own essential Life. Created beings have no holiness. The gods of the heathen have not holiness inherent in their conception. They are only to be conceived of by their worshippers as enshrining certain powers which they personify. The Name of our God is great and awful because it has this holiness essentially inherent within it. The holiness of the Three Persons is not a multiplied holiness, but a communicated holiness which as a living power loses nothing by its communication. It is one and the same holiness in each of the Three.

b. God hath done great things for Mary, great things for mankind, by taking the substance of man into personal union with the holy Substance of God, so that manhood henceforth shall live with the glory of the Only-begotten. Before the Incarnation manhood was in various degrees the recipient of overshadowing influences from God. Now the Body of Christ is a radiating principle of Divine Holiness. Mary, in contemplating the Child whom she bore in her womb, could not but express the worship which she gave to Him, by acknowledging the holiness of that Almighty Presence.

c. She had been sanctified that He might take to Himself a body of her substance. That which is conceived in her is a holy thing, for it is the body of Him whose name is Holy. The substance taken from her and living with the life of nature is taken into God that it may live with the holiness of the Almighty.

3. *Mary worshipping her Child.*

a. The greatness thus enshrined in the Child whom she bore makes her conscious of her own nothingness, just in proportion to the nearness into which she is brought with His Divine Majesty. So must it ever be. The more we are brought into the living presence of the Divine greatness, the more must we learn our nothingness. While somewhat separates us from God, we feel ourselves to be somewhat. Self disappears as God is increasingly revealed. Self·shall be lost when God shall be known as all in all.

b. The greatness of God's Name brought home to our consciousness as we become partakers of His life, must make us feel increasingly indifferent to all that is accidental, earthly, belonging only to the faculties of nature. Our only greatness is to know His greatness, to minister to His manifestation, that nothing of ourselves may mar the glory of His self-sufficing majesty.

c. Our littleness cannot hinder the greatness of His manifestation if we are conscious of our own nothingness, and lose all thought of self in praising the Divine holiness of His sovereign power. Great gifts of nature are apt to puff up and to destroy those who possess them. The great gifts of grace necessitate our being absorbed as we receive them in the contemplation of the great, the awful, the holy Name of Him to whom they belong.

IX.

τὸ ἔλεος αὐτοῦ εἰς γενεὰς γενεῶν τοῖς φοβουμένοις αὐτόν.

His mercy is unto all generations for them that fear Him.

The Discriminating Character of the Divine Goodness.

1. God's mercy a self-communicating holiness.
2. The abiding character of God's covenant.
3. The conditions of our admission.

1. *His mercy.*

a. The holiness of God separates Him from the sinful creature. And yet this holiness is the very bond which binds Him to them. It is no mere dead holiness like the imaginary holiness of some false object of worship from which the very worshippers shrink in terror, fearing lest it should do them evil, worshipping with deprecation rather than expecting it to do them good and worshipping with joyous hope. Even David feared to bring the ark of God to his house when he saw how the sinner wanting in faith was struck by its vengeance. But he learnt afterwards to look to it with confidence when he saw the blessing which came

upon Obed-Edom.   He needed thus to learn the
love which is the essential glory of the Divine
Holiness.

b. The Name of God whereby He makes Himself known, the grace whereby He reveals Himself,
is not a repellent power but a self-communicative
holiness.   The Love which is the interior law of
His being shows itself forth as mercy to those that
are outside.   By His Word He created them out of
nothing.   By His Word He calls them to partake
of His Divine Life.   His power created.   His
mercy invites. , His power gave a capacity of re-
cognising His goodness.   His mercy invites those
who will recognise it to share it.

c. His mercy is no mere tolerant and external
reconciliation.   His mercy which invites is a transforming power to such as accept the invitation.
His Holy Name is a life-giving power by which
the sinner is raised out of the death of sin and
made to live with the very Life of the Divine Holiness.   Those who receive the Word are admitted
into the Covenant of His Name so as to become
the sons of God.   His mercy is not the veiling of
His justice, but the communication of His righteousness.

2. *Its endurance.*

a. The mercy of God is no mere occasional act.
It is His essential and unchanging characteristic.
It cannot cease as long as His work of creation

continues.   Its breadth is to include all the world, its length to continue throughout all generations of mankind.   Nor is it transitory in its operation towards those who receive it.   God has given unto us eternal Life in His Son.

b. All generations partake of its blessing while they are on earth, and are gathered into its imperishable glory when they leave this world. They do not merely rejoice in successive experiences. They shall rejoice all together in collective fruition. Before Christ came there had been various manifestations of God's temporal mercy in His government of the chosen people, but mercy had been followed by judgment.   That which had been mercifully preserved was upon misconduct justly taken away.   Now, however, the holiness of God's Name is manifested in the spiritual, eternal mercy of redeeming love.   This is unchanging.   It develops in fresh gifts of power which only show more and more what its truth is.   ' He hath delivered us from death and doth deliver.   In Him we trust that He will yet deliver us ' (2 Cor. i. 10).

c. His mercy never expends itself. He is unwearied in the bounty whereby He seeks to bring men to Himself.   Their various provocations, instead of driving Him back, do but develop in successive generations the manifoldness of His inventive power.   He is ever adapting Himself to meet their needs and overcome the variety of their transgressions.

3. *Its conditions.*

a. None can profit by His mercy but those who fear His justice. 'The fear of the Lord is the beginning of wisdom.' None can escape from evil but those who hate it. None can hate evil unless they fear God. Evil is not repulsive in itself to the natural heart. It is only repulsive by reason of its consequences. We do not fear the Lord because we fear the evil consequences which may naturally follow from any evil conduct. We fear Him when we recognise the antagonism of His holiness to our inherent sinfulness. We fear Him when we would accept any outward evil rather than come into antagonism with His Holiness such as our sin deserves. He communicates holiness whereby we may be transformed, and they that fear Him would seek to die to themselves in order that they may not die to His transforming Love.

b. The mercy of God does not therefore lead to presumption, but to reverence. If God were not merciful as He is, we could not fear Him, for we should be necessarily the objects of His vengeance. We can only fear that whose operation is contingent. We do not fear the inevitable. God's mercy wakens our fear, because we have been made partakers of a benefit which by transgression of His covenant we may yet forfeit. So do we 'fear the Lord and His goodness' (Hos. iii. 5).

c. God's justice is the object of hatred to the damned. God's mercy is the object of fear to the redeemed. He whose Name is Holy calls us mercifully to partake of His Holiness that we may abide in His Love.

X.

ἐποίησε κράτος ἐν βραχίονι αὐτοῦ.
He hath showed strength with His arm.

𝔊𝔥𝔯𝔦𝔰𝔱 𝔱𝔥𝔢 𝔄𝔯𝔪 𝔬𝔣 𝔱𝔥𝔢 𝔏𝔬𝔯𝔡.

1. A Personal Ruler.
2. His power no earthly power.
3. The manifestation of the Creator.

1. *God's Sovereignty.*

a. The great things which God accomplished by the Incarnation have been already considered. Now the Blessed Virgin contemplates the sovereignty of God, the authoritative power which He exercises in His kingdom. The mercy of God belongs to Him as a sovereign. A mere power is not merciful. It may be dangerous if exerted, but it is simply harmless if tranquil. God is merciful because He is the Righteous Judge. The reason why we should fear Him is that we have violated the legitimate claim of His sovereignty. The praise of God's mercy is therefore introductory to the praise of God's sovereignty.

b. Men act against the sovereignty of God

whenever the rebellious heart cries out in fear of
vengeance.   The imprisoned spirit can only look
up to God and cry, 'Let us cast away His cords
from us.'   The cry is futile.   The loving soul
looks up to Him and owns the justice of whatever
He may appoint in the way of chastisement.

c. If we fear Him, we shall not fear the discipline to which He subjects us.   We shall feel
assured that His sovereign power is ordering all
for our real good, however painful may be the
events of the moment.   'Though I go through the
valley of the shadow of death, I will fear no evil,
for Thou art with me.'   God's sovereignty is our
constant ground of confidence.   If we are fearing
Him, we know His eye is upon us and He will
show us His covenanted mercy.   Whatever powers
may be ranged against us, we know they are all
subordinate to Him and cannot harm us save by
the permission of His Love who will turn that
seeming harm to eventual and everlasting good.

2. *The display of sovereignty.*

a. God displays His sovereignty by the very
secrecy of His operations.   'The kingdom of God
cometh not by observation.'   If He used the great
powers of nature for the accomplishment of His
designs in grace, then His kingdom would seem
to be an outgrowth of this present world. He makes
the Divine character of His sovereign acts to be
beyond dispute by using things for purposes alto-

gether beyond and even contrary to their natural capacity. A virgin from a despised village becomes the mother of Him who is to rule the world with a rod of iron. The people round about her do not know what now has happened, but the birth of her Child shall be the date by which all the chronology of the world shall be regulated. This birth is a turning-point in the world's history.

b. Other sovereigns may have lived so as to mark epochs by their accession to power, but such events are only of local interest after all. This birth is an event which, although absolutely unnoticed by the people that were around, shall be remembered in every place through future ages; for it is the coming into the world of the Sovereign who is no mere conqueror of certain hostile tribes, founding a dynasty which after a time will pass away, but He is the Conqueror of the enemy of mankind, and His sovereign power will be ready to aid all throughout all future generations who fly to Him for protection.

c. The Child that shall be born is so truly the Incarnation of Divine Sovereignty that all who would seek His benefits must personally come to Him to receive them, and none who come to Him shall go away unsatisfied. In proportion as His sovereignty is acknowledged the nations of the world will find blessing. His law, uttered by His own lips to casual throngs in a remote province of the empire, shall become the basis of the world's

moral regeneration, and none of His words shall
fall to the ground. The Divine character of the
sovereignty of Christ is to be evidenced by the
very scorn which surrounds Him even in spite of
the miracles which He works. The hatred of
man cannot make His words powerless, for He
that speaks is the Sovereign of the world, the
Lord of life, and of His kingdom there shall be
no end. He does not receive power from earth.
He brings to earth the power of God, a power inherent in Himself.

3. *The arm of the Lord.*

a. The sovereignty of God is manifested in such
a way that men will be unwilling to acknowledge
it. Being simply and purely Divine, it cannot be
perceived by any human faculty. It can only be
known by its eventual developments, and in itself
could not be recognised save by the intimations of
prophetic utterance which hearts devout and pure
delight to reflect upon. Such hearts can see that
this is He of whom prophets spake, but the worldly
heart ' sees in Him no beauty to make Him to be
desired.' This is ' the Arm of the Lord. To whom
shall He be revealed ? for He shall grow up before
Him as a tender plant, and as a root out of the dry
ground.'

b. The sovereignty of God is manifested in
the Incarnation, for this Child is He by whom all
God's acts have been done. He is no mere angel

E

so as to be an instrument in God's hand. He is the very Arm of God acting with personal authority in the fulness of Divine Life. That Arm takes hold of human nature, and, clothing itself therewith, acts through the feebleness of man so as to display the inherent power of God. He acts in His own Name, for He is consubstantial with the Father.

c. The Arm which upholds the Universe is come near, so that by taking upon Himself our nature He may act as man among men, assuming our feebleness but not forfeiting His own sovereignty. He loses nothing by taking upon Himself our nothingness, for He does not separate Himself from the Eternal Father. Though He acts for a season in the emptiness of the flesh which He assumes, He remains nevertheless indissolubly united with the Father, and the actions wrought in His humiliation are done by the power of the Holy Ghost resting upon Him in the fulness of Divine unction, so that even when He shall die, having subjected Himself to the conditions of fallen humanity, He shall yet live and triumph in the very act of death by the fulness of the power of God.

XI.

διεσκόρπισεν ὑπερηφάνους ἐν διανοίᾳ καρδίας αὐτῶν.
He hath scattered the proud in the imagination of their hearts.

𝔗𝔥𝔢 𝔇𝔢𝔰𝔱𝔯𝔲𝔠𝔱𝔦𝔬𝔫 𝔬𝔣 𝔱𝔥𝔢 𝔘𝔫𝔟𝔢𝔩𝔦𝔢𝔳𝔦𝔫𝔤.

1. The pride of the natural heart.
2. The scattering which awaits it.
3. The deceitfulness of that whereon it relies.

1. *The proud,* i.e., the scornful and unbeliev-ing [=לצים Prov. iii. 34; James iv. 6; 1 Peter v. 5].

a. The pride here intended is the pride of the natural heart which refuses to accept the control of God's law. So in Ps. i. 1, 'The seat of the scornful.' 'Boasters, *proud,* blasphemers.' Not so much referring to social pride, although that is involved, but primarily to the self-satisfied, self-reliant opposition to God in the natural heart.

b. How does the Incarnation set at nought the preconceived imaginations of mankind! God whom they proudly set aside appears in the midst of them in such a way that they can treat His manifestation with as much scorn as they treated

His absence. The unbelieving would drive us from our faith by their mockery, but we must not be surprised at their taunts. ' The proud have *scorned* me (had me greatly in derision), yet have I not shrinked from Thy Law.'

c. The acceptance of Christ requires a humble and reverent attitude of the soul towards God. His ways are not as our ways, and if we lay down the conditions upon which He should act we shall find ourselves rejecting His action, because He does not fulfil those conditions. So it is with all God's dealings towards us in His Church. ' There is no beauty that we should desire Him.' We must accustom ourselves to accept from God what is most contrary to our natural idea of fitness.

d. He fulfils His promises in ways that we cannot anticipate, and the fulfilment turns to the condemnation of the unbelieving. As the captain who scorned Elisha's prophecy received the prophecy against himself, ' Behold, thou shalt see with thine eyes but shalt not eat thereof,' so do the unbelieving receive God's gifts only to perish thereby. We must be blind to our own imaginations, knowing our incapacity, if we would see God's work of grace and learn the greatness of His power. The work of pride begins with greatness and ends in littleness. The work of God begins in ways imperceptible, and overmasters in the end all who refuse to reverence its hidden operations.

2. *The scattering.*

a. The Incarnation is a principle of mysterious unity to those who receive its power, and it brings to nought every kind of unity that is based upon worldly power. It scatters the proud. As God of old scattered the proud builders of Babel, confounding their language, so He scatters those who would build up worldly schemes of earthly wisdom, speaking to them by His word in such a form that they understand it not. Even the sheep may for a time be scattered because the Shepherd is smitten. Yet must we return to the Good Shepherd, and stand beside His cross and die with Him to all our worldly imaginations.

b. The enemies of the Lord shall be scattered as chaff and as smoke (Ps. i. 4, lxviii. 2), however powerful and united they may seem for a season. The breath of the Lord is an unseen power to scatter the ungodly who rely upon some worldly foundation, and to infuse life even into dry bones which lie about in the valley, so that they become one.

c. We must not fear though we be scattered in the world. The day is coming when the Shepherd will seek His flock among the sheep that are scattered (Ezek. xxxiv. 12). The scattering of providential discipline is for the purposes of love. It is the scattering from the presence of the Lord (Ps. lxviii. 1) in the great day that is to be feared.

'The day of the Lord shall be upon all that is proud and haughty, and upon all that is lifted up' (Is. ii. 12). They must all be scattered that are not 'rooted and built up in Him,' so as to abide in Him whom they have loved unseen, and share His glory in the day of revelation.

3. *The mode of the scattering.*

a. The faithful may be scattered by God's power for purposes of love. They learn thereby their weakness. The proud are scattered by the very success of what they have devised. That whereon they rely is used by God's power to be the instrument of their destruction. Their understanding is darkened by the sinfulness of their heart. They devise what they desire and become blind to what God wills. They 'fulfil the desires of their flesh and of their imaginations' (Eph. ii. 3), 'and so they have their imagination darkened' (Eph. iv. 18). Thus blinded to God they welcome to themselves the very things which become their destruction.

b. Our prayer must be to have 'the eyes of our imagination enlightened by the spirit of wisdom and revelation in the knowledge of Him' (Eph. i. 18). But this cannot be save by the exercise of the Spirit. 'The natural man cannot receive the things of the Spirit of God.' By purity of imagination giving heed to the words of prophecy, we must be on our guard against the scoffers, the proud (2 Pet. iii. 1, 2). It is by moral endeavour that we are to shake off the deceits of the flesh, 'girding up the loins of our imagination, and hoping soberly to the end for the grace that is being brought to us in the revelation of Jesus Christ' (1 Pet. i. 13).

c. False beliefs are a judgment upon the moral guilt of earthly self-confidence. We can only be safe while we walk with God. ' I have more understanding than the aged, because I keep Thy statutes. Let the proud be confounded, for they go wickedly about to destroy me. Let such as fear Thee and have known Thy testimonies be turned unto me. Let my heart be sound in Thy statutes that I be not ashamed ' (Ps. cxix. 100, 78, 79, 80). 'He hath given us a' spiritual 'imagination that we may know Him that is true' (1 John v. 20). ' All the imaginations of the thoughts of man's heart are only evil continually' (Gen. vi. 5). But we must love the Lord our God with all our imagination (Matt. xxii.). The only thought of our heart must be to love Him in the power of the renewing Spirit of Love.

XII.

καθεῖλε δυνάστας ἀπὸ θρόνων.
He hath put down the mighty from thrones.

The Overthrow of the Powers of Darkness.

1. The Prince of this world and his powers.
2. The thrones they occupy.
3. The presence of Christ the Conqueror.

1. *The potentates.*

a. These are the powers of darkness, the spirits of evil that tyrannise over the world. They appear in the Old Testament as presiding over the heathen nations, and are in antagonism to Michael the Prince of the covenanted people. We are not to think of their power as if it were now at an end. They are not dependent upon the natural world which they organise. They have spiritual strength, which they infuse into the material organism in order to carry out the purposes of evil, while they possess a knowledge of the secrets of nature altogether surpassing what we know, so that they are able to contend with us in twofold strength. They are doubtless all of them confederated under the headship of Satan as the Prince of this world. Formed for heavenly action, they have capacity of simulating heavenly power. They can clothe themselves as angels of light, although their inward being is always darkness. They can thus attract to themselves the homage of mankind, so as to deceive by lying wonders and specious pretexts of good even the very elect. Their whole existence is falsehood, being at variance with God who is Truth.   Satan is ' a liar and the father of it.'

b. They have power in this lower world because it has been given to them by God. So Satan himself says to Christ. Therefore they retain this power until they are cast into the abyss. We must not be surprised, then, if we find evil triumphing in the world. We must rather be suspicious of that which triumphs by worldly power. We must not be afraid of worldly power, for it is deceptive and will soon pass away.

c. If we would have abiding power, we must 'continue in the truth.' 'The truth makes us free' from the bondage of these lying spirits.   'He that committeth sin is the servant of sin,' for the powers of darkness claim dominion over him, and even communicate to him their nature by diabolical inspiration, so that they become children of the devil. The seed of the serpent is at enmity with

the seed of the woman.   How carefully must we,
as being 'born of God, keep ourselves so that the
evil one may not touch us!'   How must we bring
all things to the test of God's revelation!   How
vain it is for us to contend with Satan!   All we
can do is to say, 'The Lord rebuke thee!' commit-
ting ourselves to Him that judgeth righteously,
and assured that, however evil may seem to pro-
sper in the world, we may 'commit the keeping of
our souls to God in well-doing as to a faithful
Creator' (1 Pet. iv. 19).

 d. Surrounded by the powers of darkness, ever
ready to deceive and overthrow, how must we rest
secure simply in God's love, looking up to Him
with constant prayer!   The proud, unbelieving
scoffers perish through the powers which sway
the world, but which are to them unseen.   We
need not be afraid of the powers of darkness if we
are abiding in the power of God.

 2. *The thrones.*

 a. The hierarchy of spiritual wickedness is
organised according to God's creative will.   What
their position was when He created them in His
eternal truth, that their position remains although
they have lost the light of truth.   They held the
world in subjection until their tyranny was set
aside.   They raised men up to be their vicegerents
and outward agents.   How must we contemplate

their thrones now vacant in heaven, waiting to be filled by the redeemed!

b. Man, though created in subjection to angels, will judge angels in the end. Jesus mounts from the cross to the throne of glory, and they who suffer shall reign with Him.

c. We must not be eager to climb to any thrones of power in this present dispensation. Not until the world to come is made manifest, shall we acquire the kingdom. It is ' our Father's good pleasure to give it to the little flock,' but not until the enemy has been cast into the lake of fire. Then shall we reign with Christ for ever and ever. Then shall the redeemed occupy the place from which the angels fell, and the original order of God's predestination shall be restored with added glory through the manifestation of Divine Life in Christ.

3. *The overthrow.*

a. Christ puts down the powers of darkness from their thrones by His own appearance. No created power could do this, for they were constituted on their thrones by the will of the Creator. The Word who gave them their dignity becomes incarnate so as to accomplish their punishment and effect their overthrow. In the heavenly places He acts as in the earthly vineyard. ' He miserably destroys those wicked ones and gives the vineyard to others.' How must we look to Him as an inexorable Judge!

b. No benefits that we have received can warrant us in presuming upon the continuance of His favour. We have been called to fill the place from which beings much mightier than ourselves fell away. We cannot be secure unless we abide in Him who is the Truth. We cannot claim the kingdom by our own right, nor seize it by our own power, nor retain it by our own sufficiency. 'Abide in Me and let My words abide in you.' So Christ speaks. We must look to him as the Conqueror of Satan. He it is who shall 'tread down Satan under our feet shortly.'

c. How must we despise every semblance of earthly power! Yea, how must we tremble if we possess it! It matters not of what kind it be, material or spiritual. Christ puts down all who look to any position of this world. Christ puts all down by the power of the Holy Ghost. Whatever is high and lifted up must perish before Him. The Lord alone shall be exalted in that day. Whatever power assails us, we must meet it in His strength.

d. Never need we fear any because they are great. Rather let any greatness of our enemies be an encouragement. We know that it is a principle of weakness in itself. The more boastful it may be, the more sure is God to destroy it. He hears the groaning of His people in Egypt. He hears the insolence of Sennacherib. Satan appears before God to accuse the people of Christ. God may let him take from us all wherein the natural heart would delight, but it is His purpose thus to condemn sin in the flesh that we may attain to be enthroned in the glory of His holy love.

XIII.

ὕψωσεν ταπεινούς.

He hath exalted the lowly.

The Exaltation of Humanity.

1. Beyond any natural attainment.
2. The hope of the glory of God.
3. The consciousness of our present incapacity.

1. *The exaltation.*

a. As the powers of darkness are cast down from their thrones, so man is exalted to take their place. The exaltation of man is indeed to a glory even higher than that of the angels; but we must first consider it as being (what it originally is) a replacement of the fallen angels by the newly created race of man. They lost their power by resting in it, falling away from dependence upon God. The exaltation of man is not by any natural upgrowth, but by an act of Divine grace. The same Divine Love which in its justice cast down the angels by its mercy raised mankind. Our first thought must be that of wondering gratitude. Our second thought must be humble self-distrust.

b. Looking back to this original fall, we must consider the same moral law as obliging us to watchfulness. So St. Peter expressly speaks. ‹ God spared not the angels which sinned.’ If God spared not them, created as they were for this glory, ‘take heed lest He spare not thee.’ Such would be St. Paul’s warning.

c. But how much greater is this glory than the glory which man could have attained by nature ! How ought we then to look upward with an earnest longing, not letting ourselves be satisfied by any earthly conception of power, but remembering our destiny in that we are made to reign with Christ in heavenly places! How contemptible, how dangerous, how loathsome does earthly power and dignity appear to the soul which realises that it is called by grace to a dignity not of earth, but to be as the angels of God. in heaven ! Satan would have us shudder at gross material sin in order thus to deceive us. The worst sins are the sins akin to his spiritual nature, sins of intellect, sins of spirit, sins of pride. God scatters the proud, the unbelieving scorner by the very imagination of his own heart. We must accept all exaltation as being His simple gift. We must exercise all gifts of honour as belonging simply to Him.

2. *The greater exaltation.*

a. ‘ Where sin abounded grace did much more abound.’ God has exalted man not only to occupy the thrones of fallen angels, but to sit with Himself upon the eternal throne of the Divine Life. A destiny of glorious elevation was promised to Adam if he had continued faithful. That elevation was compatible with, and therefore worthy of, the indwelling Spirit of Life, worthy of the Divine Image which Adam bore. Nothing could be worthy of that image save the glory coequal with the Father. It was veiled for a time, but it would seem as if creation without this final development of glory would have been a toy unworthy of God. All things were created for the Only-begotten Son, whose coming in the flesh had been foreordained.

b. The fall of the angels necessitated His coming as a conqueror. Adam was created to win the battle of God. Adam's fall necessitated Christ's coming in humiliation as a sufferer. Nevertheless the purpose of God standeth sure. Now the promise is accomplished.

c. By the very fact of God humbling Himself to the form of a servant, the servant's form is raised to the participation of the Divine Substance. It is an accomplished fact. 'He hath exalted.' He has taken man's nature into God. The exaltation of our nature in Christ must be to us a principle of constant watchfulness united with Divine adoration of Him who is our Head. 'Watch ye; stand fast in the faith.'

d. The participation of the Divine nature thus

given to us must be a ground not of empty assu-
rance, but of increased responsibility, 'Take heed
that ye despise not Him that speaketh from
heaven. Take heed lest there be in any of you an
evil heart of unbelief in departing from the living
God.'

3. *The lowly.*

a. God has exalted mankind, who were not
only by nature lower than the angels, but by the
Fall had become even lower than themselves, having
forfeited their predestination by becoming slaves
to sin. The exaltation of grace is above the
natural development of nature. The exaltation of
grace is a gift which not only raises man, as he
was intended to be raised, even to the glory of
God, but raises him out of his state of degradation
as a bondslave to God's great rebel involved in all
the misery of sin.

b. If we are to be partakers of the exaltation,
we must have a full sense of the degradation.
The Incarnation brings the Divine glory into
human nature, but it does not communicate the
Divine glory to any individual man.

c. We cannot have that glory save by coming
with lowly penitence and faith to be incorporated
in the renewed and renewing humanity of Christ.
No nearness of kinship by nature, though we were
as near to Him by nature as the Blessed Virgin
Mary was, no clearness of spiritual intuition,

F

though we apprehended the truth as clearly as the devils did who cried out that they knew Him, would avail. We must know ourselves to be verily, and indeed ' by nature, children of wrath.' So must each man come to Christ. We are reborn by grace in the covenant of holy baptism. ' As many as received Him, to them gave He power to become the sons of God.'

XIV.

πεινῶντας ἐνέπλησεν ἀγαθῶν.
He hath filled the hungry with good things.

𝔗𝔥𝔢 𝔖𝔞𝔱𝔦𝔰𝔣𝔞𝔠𝔱𝔦𝔬𝔫 𝔬𝔣 𝔐𝔞𝔫'𝔰 𝔑𝔢𝔢𝔡.

1. Man's hunger after righteousness.
2. The fulness of God.
3. The sweetness of Divine nourishment.

1. *The hunger after righteousness.*

a. The seat of the scornful where the proud are content to sit with Satan is contrasted with the thrones in Heaven where the lowly are called to sit with Christ. Mankind are again divided into two classes—the hungering, and the rich. Hunger implies the conscious desire of something which we have not got, for which our nature craves, without which we die. If we are to profit by Christ's coming, we must have this hunger after the righteousness which He gives.

b. We are subjected to hunger by the Fall, for we have lost by nature the supernatural endow-

F 2

ments by which alone the desire of our souls created in God's image can be satisfied. The soul has o rest outside of God, no sense of completeness unless we are   ade complete in Him. It is not man's misery to hunger. Rather it is his glory.   Man's greatest misery is to seek to feed himself with the husks of created pleasure, whereas all things round about him have lost the power of giving him what he needs, since the Divine Life has been withdrawn from all.

c. Our nature leads us to crave for Divine sustenance because God gave it to man before the Fall. We have therefore a consciousness of having lost our necessary food. Hunger is a testimony of healthy action, but the hungry die of inanition. So, the more true we are to nature, the more we feel ourselves to be perishing. 'A Syrian ready to perish was my father.' So the Israelite spake constantly. This gave thankfulness to his devotion. But there was in the Law 'no honour so as to fill the craving of the flesh.'

d. Without the gift of the Spirit of God renewing us to Divine Life, we die. Death becomes complete. Let us praise God if we feel the craving. It is no cause for indignation that we are left to feel it for a while. By feeling this hunger we become capable of being nourished. The heavenly food cannot otherwise be assimilated by us. O blessed hunger! Let me feel this more and more! I must die by this hunger to nature, that I may behold God's likeness and may be satisfied, feeding upon the beatific vision.

2. *The fulness.*

a. The fulness of God dwells in Christ, and of His fulness have all we received. Man's nature created in God's Image has not merely such an emptiness that it must die unless it be sustained by a Divine Grace; the fulness is correspondent with the emptiness. Every faculty of our nature has become empty by the Divine withdrawal.

b. Every faculty of our nature receives its corresponding fulness by the infusion of the glorified Humanity of Christ wherein dwells all the fulness of the Godhead bodily. We are not merely sustained in a life of nature satisfied with itself, but we are filled with a Theandric Life. The exaltation given to the lowly communicates itself gradually to those who hunger after the righteousness of God.

c. That righteousness does not allay the hunger by its primary communication, but glorifies the nature as we feed upon it with continual appetite. The fulness is given already, but it needs to be individualised by the life of faith that thus we may grow in holiness. Thus 'Christ is formed within us.' The fulness is entirely the gift of Christ. He is both the Giver and the Gift.

d. Human nature is the culminating object of creation. Only through man can the vanity of the creature be done away. All were created so as to be saved by the hope which should be fulfilled in man. Thus does God in Christ satisfy even the hunger of a world outside of human nature. 'He chargeth even His angels with folly,' but to them through the Church as Christ's Body 'shall be made known the manifold Wisdom of God.'

3. *The good things.*

a. Goodness is *one* with the substantial unity of God. Goodness is *manifold* with the variety of created experiences. How imperfect our fragmentary apprehension of God's goodness in this present life! How glorious will be the complete apprehension, when sight and hearing and all the senses become identified in the experience of the Divine manifestation glorifying them all, so that in our very flesh, in the essence of the faculties whose blindness now shuts God off from us, we shall see God. Seeing will be hearing, and so on.

b. There will be no faculty in the risen body which does not exist for the sole purpose of apprehending God, none that fails to apprehend Him, none that does not recognise in loving fellowship of act the Divine Presence which all the other faculties of that glorious organism will also enjoy. A flood of enjoyment which does not disturb the harmony of the risen life by the passionate excitement of one faculty to the detriment of others, but

fills the whole nature with an entrancing peace-
fulness of calm delight.

    c. That delight shall not exhaust the faculties
as the passion of earthly pleasure does. It shall
sustain, nourish, perfect, glorify the whole nature
of man with the eternal joy of the communication
of God, the Spirit of Christ working in all the
members of His Body. 'The Word was made flesh
and dwelt among us,' and we are made the members of His Body, that in the Resurrection we may
dwell in Him for evermore, evermore to 'taste and
see how gracious the Lord is.'

XV.

πλουτοῦντας ἐξαπέστειλε κενούς.

The rich He hath sent empty away.

The Emptiness of Present Satisfaction.

1. The worthlessness of earthly things.
2. The dismissal of those who lived for them.
3. The eternal sense of loss.

1. *The rich.*

a. These are they whom this world call rich, who think themselves to be so, boasting of that which keeps them from the true wealth.

False riches are those which come *to* us. They seem to be means of power. They are rather burdens that weigh down the soul, dead riches.

True riches are those which come *from* us, in so far as we are ' rich towards God.'

We *are* rich by what comes to us, but these riches we lose. While we have them they are only a tomb, a prison. They help not the real living activity of the soul. They do not forward the true purpose of our being. They do not enable

us to live any the more worthy of God our Creator
or of the nature He has given us.

We *become* rich by that which comes from us,
for by acts worthy of our Divine origin in the power
of the Holy Ghost we lay up treasure in heaven.
We are raised out of the world. We make return
to God of that sanctifying Spirit which constitutes
our Life. Then we become rich with God and in
Him, for such operation of the Holy Ghost stab-
lishes us in the Being of God.

b. We are not rich toward God in proportion
to the amount we can yield to Him, but in proportion to the Divine quality of the action, the
heavenly glory of the life which fills the gift.

A restful state of being rich, as an accomplished fact, is therefore a state of absolute poverty,
a spiritual deadness. A living state of richness
not in ourselves, but towards God, is an active
state, a growing state, a state in which the
present poverty is felt by reason of the greatness
of the demand which it makes upon us.

c. It matters not of what kind the riches may
be which we possess—material, intellectual, spiritual. What is possessed as making us rich by its
possession, makes us poor by its deadness. 'Thou
sayest, I am rich, and have become rich, and have
need of nothing.' True riches cannot be attained
in this world, but are always in a state of being
attained. The riches of grace developed in the
actions of grace glorify the soul which is using

them, but in a moment of stagnation they cease to be. To feel our riches is to sink under our poverty.

2. *The sending away.*

a. It is an anticipation of the words 'Depart, ye cursed.' The Prince of this world is cast away. So too the princes of this world who held it under him. So too the Jews, God's ancient people who had the law, which should have made them rich toward God, and became impoverished by the law because they prized it as a gratification of their own pride. So shall it be with the Christian that makes boast whether of position, or of attainments, or of any power capable of external determination.

b. If we rest in the riches which are outside of God, God will send us away to experience the worthlessness of that which we delight in. We need no other curse to all eternity than to enjoy what we have lived for, and find that its enjoyment brings us no nearer to God.

c. Now we do not know what it is to be without God. In the light of Divine Providence good and bad experience many tokens of God's Love. *Hereafter* the soul that is driven away from God will find that it can only subsist in the light of God's Presence, and its curse is to be sent with that which it lived for into the darkness far away from God.

3. *Empty.*

a. Then shall the emptiness of created things at last be known. The greater has been the repletion of the riches, the more terrible will be the depletion when that emptiness shall be experienced. Unless we are now seeking the fulness of grace, we must find the emptiness of eternity. The soul which has lost God has within itself a law of eternal doom by the hunger which it shall experience.

We may have the fulness of earthly acquisition, but all these things are only manifold forms of emptiness. As they have no power in themselves, they seem but to indicate the want of that power which alone can make them of avail.

b. Empty things intensify our consciousness of being empty, serve but the more to drive away from us the fulness of God here, as they will hereafter cause us to be driven away in irredeemable emptiness from the fulness of God's Glory.

Those who hunger after God and feel their poverty shall be increasingly filled with His presence while they use His Grace. Those who rejoice in the riches of nature must learn the emptiness of nature.

c. Nothing can be filled with God which is not given to God, for the Holy Ghost does not come to us as a river dashing over a precipice to flow onward to the sea. The Holy Ghost is a power which comes to us from God, fills us with God, and carries us back by His necessary circulating power to God as the final object of our being.

We must thus be drawn to God in the fulness of grace, or we must be cast away from God, having relied upon the riches of nature to find the emptiness of a state of banishm ent from Him.

XVI.

ἀντελάβετο Ἰσραὴλ παιδὸς αὐτοῦ.[1]

He hath holpen His servant Israel.

𝕿𝖍𝖊 𝕮𝖔𝖛𝖊𝖓𝖆𝖓𝖙𝖊𝖉 𝕽𝖊𝖑𝖆𝖙𝖎𝖔𝖓𝖘𝖍𝖎𝖕.

1. The Divine Prince.
2. The elect servant.
3. The help which God gives.

1. *Israel.*

a. The title points to the victory of Jacob during the night of wrestling. He became a prince with God and left his claim to his posterity. However negligent Israel might be of their prerogatives, God was not forgetful of them. The results of that victory could not be transferred to any other nation. 'I will not let Thee go unless Thou bless *me*.' That blessing must be given. There was but one blessing to give, and that blessing was the Incarnation of the Son of God. All blessings are summed up in Him. The nation

---

[1] Cf. Isaiah xli. 9, σὺ δὲ Ἰσραήλ, παῖς μου, Ἰακώβ, καὶ ὃν ἐξελεξάμην σπέρμα Ἀβραάμ, ὃν ἠγάπησα, οὗ ἀντελαβόμην ἀπ᾽ ἄκρων τῆς γῆς.

which had the prerogative that 'of them as concerning the flesh Christ should come who is over all God blessed for ever,' stood in a position quite unique amongst the nations of the world. God could not but look upon them with an interest which He could take in no other. That nation was a Prince with God for evermore.

2. *The servant of God.*

a. Israel was the Servant of God, the Child of God, in a special manner, not merely by an ideal elevation, a national consecration, but by the personal relationship that the Incarnation would involve. The prophecies which belong to Israel belong to Christ. If the prophecies which belong to Christ have any preparatory fulfilment in Israel, it is because of the foreseen relationship; not by any arbitrary, or idealising, substitution, but by a reality of kindred and personal identification. Their historical accomplishment is a typical event leading onward to the personal fulfilment.

The word 'servant' implies not merely the slavish service from which Israel, by reason of a Divine necessity, could not escape, but the filial service in which Israel as the elect Son of God was to rejoice. The law was a schoolmaster to bring them to Christ, and the prophets were to arouse them not to any mere boast of human consciousness, but to the Christian consciousness of the glory of Him who was to come. He when He came would raise them to a Divine glory.

b. Christ was to take upon Himself the form of a servant, and He is the only servant who has fulfilled or could fulfil the duties required of such a relationship. The law which was given required a service which none could yield. It required the fulness of Divine Life. It was the portraiture of the Righteousness of God.

c. To be elect to so high a service implied election to the corresponding relationship. God did not give commands to Israel merely in irony, mocking their weakness, but in love, pledging Himself thus to the communication of power. 'This do, and thou shalt live. I will give thee strength to do it.'

So with us now, every high vocation with its special difficulties is a pledge of corresponding grace. Therefore, if God gives us any command we may always make answer, 'I am able. I can do all things through God which strengtheneth me.'

3. *He hath holpen.*

a. The help which God gives is the help of an eternal life. The Hebrew leads us to the stricter interpretation *He hath laid hold of.* It is not quite the same, but very nearly what is said in

Hebrews (ii. 16), 'He laid hold of the seed of Abraham.' This phrase rather implies the help which He gives Israel by becoming the substitute for Israel's infirmities. The phrase in the Hebrews indicates principally His personal participation in that nature which He assumes. Christ is the *strong* Hand, the Hand Whose helpful strength cannot fail. The carpenter strengthened his work with nails, but God strengthens Israel with Divine Life (Is. xli. 7–9).

b. That strength foreseen was a pledge of security during all the ages of weakness. God strengthened Israel with a watchful love, a love which must at length show itself in Divine power. What advantage then had they? We can see how true an answer is given by St. Paul, *Much every way.* It was not the external advantages which they possessed which raised them in the scale of nations. On the contrary they were to experience antagonisms and overthrow altogether beyond their strength to endure, beyond what any nation of the world would know. But there was a mysterious vitality in Israel, and that vitality was to show itself in due time. Israel must live until Messiah comes. Messiah is the life of Israel. The hopes of Israel are to be realised in Him. He was to be *of* Israel. Henceforth Israel is to be found only *in* Him. He is 'born of a woman, born under the law to redeem them that were under the law,' not that they should remain in the weakness of their natural condition, but that they might receive the adoption of sons. 'As many as received Him, to them gave He power to become the sons of God.'

XVII.

μνησθῆναι ἐλέους.

So as to remember His mercy.

The Remembered Mercy.

1. The character of mercy.
2. Its recipients.
3. God's changeless purpose.

1. *Mercy.*

a. The race which looks for God's redemption must look for it as an act of mercy. There was no claim of justice. Love had been forfeited. Mercy must remove the barrier which original sin had interposed between God and the nature which He would assume, the chosen race to which He would give His help.

Hannah speaks of God's judgments. Mercy is not the mere deliverance from evils now experienced. It is the power enabling man to meet the judgment to which he will be eventually subjected.

b. Mercy is not mere pity which alleviates suffering, but it is a gift empowering man to

accomplish that which the Judge requires. ' Mercy
and Truth meet together.' Mercy without truth
were no mercy at all. Mercy therefore here anti-
cipates the saying of St. John, that *grace and truth
came by Jesus Christ*. Mercy consists in that gift
of grace and truth which the Incarnation involves.

2. *The recipients of mercy.*

a. In this word Mary acknowledges herself as
belonging to a sinful race, as she has already done
by the word Saviour. It were no mercy to be
exempted from original sin, for the non-existent
being is incapable of receiving mercy, and whatever may be the prerogatives of our birth, requir-
ing our gratitude to God as our Creator, we cannot
call them by the name of mercy. That which is
nothing has neither worthiness nor unworthiness.
God of His good pleasure can create a being with
whatever endowments He pleases. Mercy implies
that the recipient had an *inherent unworthiness* of
the bounty which is shown.

b. The truth of our Lord's Godhead quickens
the mercy wherewith He raises our nature out of
the consequences of the Fall. The act of mercy
consists in His thus taking hold of His servant
Israel by the grasp of the Divine nature wherewith He restores humanity to its true life. The
moment of the Incarnation is therefore the beginning of this mercy, not any previous moment
which might be conceived as making man fit to

receive it. Prophets told of the coming mercy which Christ brought. In proportion as man was made fit to receive it, the quality of mercy would be itself destroyed. What we are fit to receive we receive as an act of justice, not of mercy, but man never could be fitted to receive the gift of the Incarnation and the deliverance from sin which it involves.

c. We are fitted to receive mercy simply by the fact that we are sinners perishing unless we receive it. We must therefore take encouragement. No sin unfits us to receive God's mercy. 'Him that cometh to Me I will in no wise cast out.' He that has been four days dead is as capable of being raised to life as any other that died but an hour ago. 'As therefore we have received mercy, we faint not.'

3. *The memory of God.*

a. God remembers His mercy, for He does not act upon any mere sudden emotion awakened by the sight of man's misery. He keeps to the purpose which He has had for mankind, coeval with the original fall. God did not suffer man to fall that man might perish, but that He might be glorified by the exercise of mercy towards man. Were it not for this mercy, God's purpose in man's creation would have been frustrated, but 'mercy rejoiceth over judgment.' Such mercy is not the mere setting aside of judgment and justifying the sinner, but it is justifying the sinner so that he may meet the requirements of the judgment.

b. The Incarnation and Atonement are no afterthought, but they are a part of that dispensation of love which created man with a moral nature capable of rising up to the Divine love— capable not in itself, but by the assistance of a higher power to be communicated when the natural incapacity had been proved.

c. If the trial of man's love had not been too great for human nature, it would not have been adequate to the requirement of Divine Love. It must be seen that man had failed naturally to deserve that Love. Then God would give supernatural grace so that man might rise to its requirement and acquire it. No love can be worthy of God which is not Divine, but man is made capable of loving God with a Divine Love by the communication of the Spirit of Christ. Thus did God determine that man should receive His mercy, and be raised to a position wherein he might be fit for the Divine Love.

d. God had watched the nations of mankind through various temptations and failures, but He always looked forward to sending His Son with grace sufficient to meet all the requirements of every individual of the human race. So ' when the fulness of time was come, He sent His Son.' He remembered His mercy, and helped His servant Israel. Man's sin was manifest, but God looked beneath man's sin to the glorious being which He had predestinated to be conformed to His own Image and share His glory. So the Psalmist sings, *O remember not the sins and offences of my youth, but according to Thy mercy remember me, O Lord, for Thy goodness.*

XVIII.

καθὼς ἐλάλησε πρὸς τοὺς πατέρας ἡμῶν.
As He spake to our fathers.

The Patriarchal Expectation.

1. The necessity of prophecy.
2. God's faithfulness to His Covenant.
3. The memory of the past.

1. *The necessity of Prophecy.*

a. Whatever God's purpose might have been, we could not have recognised it unless it had been announced beforehand. God made known the pre-destined salvation so that the previous generations might look forward to the coming of Christ in order to prepare for it, and we might acknowledge its truth so as to receive it now that it has come.

b. It was impossible that man should recognise the voice of God if God had come amongst us in the ordinary way of human action. If He had borne witness of Himself alone His witness could not have been received as true. Nor could we have given due faith to any miraculous actions if God had simply appeared amongst us in the exercise of powers greater than belong to man. It was needful that the Incarnation should be accomplished with attendant miracles as befitted the approach of God, and that there should be a previous expectation of such accomplishment resting upon the credentials of antecedent religion. The very errors mingled with the expectation testified to the truth of the fulfilment which so far surpassed it.

God therefore spake unto the fathers by prophets. They who were approved in their lifetime by many Divine tokens pointed onward to One who should claim the fulness of Divine honour.

c. The message of prophecy grew to its completeness as the appointed time drew near. Utterances which seem to be contradictory were to find their accomplishment in the birth of the Son of God, and their very contradictions would serve to corroborate the truth of His mission, since all that seemed to defy reconciliation was brought into a harmonious completeness by the circumstances of His Life.

d. When all had been announced which God thought fit, there was to be a silence of prophecy which should make the outburst of the Divine Word at the period of the Incarnation the more remarkable. Yet had God also specially marked the time, place, and manner of the Incarnation so that we might not have to rely upon any merely human testimony when the time should come, but might recognise the fulfilment of all, even as God had spoken to the fathers.

2. *God's faithfulness to His Covenant.*

a. Many generations had passed away. God had from time to time spoken. Successive generations had been constantly rebellious. Frequently had God visited their sin with renewed chastisement. Nevertheless God would not take His lovingkindness utterly from those whom He had chosen nor suffer His Truth to fail.

b. It might have seemed that a generation so miserably wanting in heavenly aspirations as the Jews were when Christ was born, might have lost all hold upon the Divine gifts. Not so. The unfaithfulness of man could not hinder the faithfulness of God. True, the heart of that generation was set on earthly things. Yet would God give the heavenly things which He had promised to their fathers. God's gift was not to be measured by their desires.

c. How must we now amidst the degradation of modern Christianity look for God's power still to assert itself in all the glory of the first manifestation! The Word of God is the same in fulfilment as it was in promise. 'Jesus Christ is the same yesterday, and to-day, and for ever.'

3. *The memory of the past.*

a. As God spake to the fathers of that which He afterwards fulfilled, so it is our duty to bear in mind what He has said, and not think that it has passed away with the generations to whom it was addressed.

b. Whatever God says is, we may be sure, a law of what God will do. God does not act with inconsistency. He has no changeable purpose. As He has revealed Himself in word to any that were before us, so we shall find Him in act towards ourselves.

c. How varied were the circumstances of our fathers! Yet was it one Divine Word leading them all onward to one great issue. So it is now. We must never think our circumstances so peculiar that we become exempted from God's Word, whether of promise or of threatening. The variations of human circumstance only serve to develop the constancy of the Divine action. If we would find ourselves capable of profiting by what God *does* we must be constantly reflecting upon what He has *said*, ' giving heed to the word of prophecy as to a light which shineth in a dark place.'

d. God makes His conduct known because we should not otherwise recognise it. Therefore His action very often seems to us to be at variance with His utterances, and it is our duty to watch for His words, and lay them up in our hearts, so that the outward events may not discourage us nor blind us to the certainty of God's final triumph. The faithful heart must see beneath the surface of events how God is accomplishing what He has said.

XIX.

τῷ ᾽Αβραὰμ καὶ τῷ σπέρματι αὐτοῦ.

For Abraham and his seed.

𝕬braham and his 𝕾eed.

1. The original covenant.
2. The Seed who should be the Heir.
3. The nature of the Blessing.

1. *The covenant with Abraham.*

a. God hath been always mindful of His covenant and promise that He made to a thousand generations, even the covenant that He made with Abraham. *To Abraham and his seed were the promises made.*

b. Prophecies had been given to the fathers, but not for their sakes. Previous generations, as those of our Lord's own day, were 'the children of the prophets and of the covenant which God made with our fathers, saying to Abraham, And in thy seed shall all the nations of the earth be blessed.' What had been said to the fathers was but the development of God's promise to Abraham.

c. It was not said for their own sakes, for they

were a stiffnecked and rebellious people from the beginning to the time of their overthrow. Nevertheless the chosen seed was amongst them. Not because they are the seed of Abraham are they all children. There must be a separation. As Isaac from Ishmael, and Jacob from Esau, so in each subsequent generation there was to be the separation going on, and at the last only 'a remnant should be saved.' So is it now. The gifts of covenanted grace profit not those who will not rise to the conditions of the covenant. 'They who are of faith shall be blessed with faithful Abraham.'

2. *Abraham's Seed.*

a. The Seed of Abraham to whom the promises are made is Christ Himself. He is the *Seed in whom all the nations of the earth shall be blessed.* He is the supernatural Seed, and no seed of Abraham which was not supernaturally born could be the channel of supernatural blessing to the nations of the world. All that were naturally born failed of fulfilling the Divine promises. The mercy of God was to be shown to the world as the prerogative of Abraham and then of Christ.

b. It might seem that Christ, who was the bringer of mercy, could not be in any sense the receiver of mercy. He brings mercy as the Son of God. He receives mercy not in His own person but in the nature transmitted to Him from Abra-

ham.   That nature had been subjected to all the
consequences of the Fall until the Son of God took
it upon Himself.   Therefore the seed or nature
of Abraham received mercy in that it was assumed
by the Son of God.   So in the Psalms Messiah
constantly speaks of salvation coming to Him.   It
comes to Him as man, because as man He is the
Heir of the promises.

   c. The dative—' for Abraham and his seed '—in
this verse is like what the Psalmist says, ' The oath
which he sware concerning Isaac.'   The mercy promised has reference to these two personages.   It
is promised to Abraham, and consummated in
Christ.

   There was no supernatural seed between Isaac
and Christ.   Isaac was supernaturally born, but
it was by a renewal of human power in his parents'
frame.   Jesus was Divinely born, the Seed of
Abraham, being sprung from him as the promised
Seed of the woman, but being born not of human
power, born of a virgin as had been prophesied to
the fathers, having no human father, for the Son of
God had not His origin from earth.   He came to
fulfil the promised mercy, being conceived by the
Holy Ghost.

   3. *The promised blessing.*

   a. What was the blessing which belonged to
Abraham and his seed, in virtue whereof all the
nations of the world were to be blessed?   It was

no gift of aggrandisement over the nations of the world by outward sovereignty. Messiah was to be the Heir of the world by becoming 'The Father of a new world' (Is. ix. 6).

b. As Isaac lived here with a new life, the parent of the chosen race, so Messiah would live with a higher Life, the parent of a new race, who by being incorporated with Him should be gathered from all the ends of the earth so as to become the children of Abraham. He would possess the world not only as servants but as children. He is the Hand wherein the staff of Judah and the staff of Israel are to become one, and when He gathered Abraham, Isaac, and Jacob, the elders of the ancient election, to sit with Him upon thrones, 'many from the east and west were to come and sit down with them in the Kingdom of Heaven' which He would establish.

c. This is that covenant of mercy to all mankind which God remembered when He sent His Son to take upon Himself our nature. In the Incarnate Son of God the seed of Abraham receives that mercy which had so long and so continuously been declared, a mercy which knows no end. This is the inheritance which Abraham was to receive when he went out not knowing whither he went. As the prophet Ezekiel gives us the measurements of the promised land, not that wherein the fathers dwelt of old, but a new, a mystical habitation, so

Abraham 'went forth looking for a city which hath foundations, whose builder and maker is God,' in a heavenly country; 'wherefore God is not ashamed to be called their God, for He hath prepared for them a city.'

XX.

εἰς τὸν αἰῶνα.

For ever.

Divine Eternity.

1. The accomplishment of Divine purposes.
2. The final deliverance.
3. The eternal Blessing.

1. *The accomplishment of Divine purposes.*

a. The help which God had promised to Israel was no merely transitory deliverance. It was a help worthy of the eternity of the Giver. God had foreseen from the beginning what He would do for Israel. From everlasting to everlasting He is God. The salvation which was to be accomplished in Israel had all along been known to Him.

b. Many another deliverance had been wrought in the interval, but all those deliverances as being transitory and typical pointed onward to that which God was purposing to do hereafter. Now the time has come.

The coming of the time was fixed by circumstances of which we have no real knowledge. We know, however, that God was waiting for *the ful-*

ness of time to be come, and when it did come then ' He sent forth His Son made of a woman, made under the law, to redeem them that were under the law, that we might receive the adoption of sons.'

c. As the entrance of Israel into the promised land was waiting for the iniquity of the Amorites to be full, so we may well conceive that the Incarnation of the Son of God was delayed until the wickedness of mankind had reached a culminating point, so that from henceforth it was manifest how utterly incapable man was to work out any deliverance for Himself.

All along God had been pointing onward to the great Deliverer.

2. *This deliverance is the final deliverance.*

a. During previous ages there had been manifold successive deliverances. These deliverances had been followed by overthrow. In the overthrow there always was a Divine certainty for the recovery of Israel. Until Christ came Israel could not pass away from among the nations of the earth. There always was the security of restoration, however great the calamity.

b. Now the history of Israel has reached its culminating point. In Messiah all nations of the earth shall be blessed, but all the glory of Israel henceforth is summed up in the Person of Messiah. This is the promised Seed of Abraham to whom the blessing belonged, and all the rest of the nations could claim the blessing only by associating themselves with Him.

c. Truly the nation through whom the blessing came to all the nations of the earth would not be excluded from the blessing which it conveyed. But all who would share this blessing must seek it from the one Person, the one Child of Abraham in whom it was inherent. Christ, the long-promised Messiah, is the beginner of a new era in history. He does not come to raise either Israel or any other nation of the earth by mere external organisation. Christ is born, the Lord of Life, to give a better life to those who shall be incorporated into Him, but without such incorporation He could not profit any. His Kingdom, though it spring up in earthly form, is to be a Kingdom of heavenly power.

3. *This deliverance is eternal.*

a. The blessing which Messiah should convey would be a blessing altogether distinct from the merely perishing phenomena of earthly nationalities. It was a blessing to all the nations of the earth. It was the blessing of a new life along with God. It was a blessing which would reach in its consequences to all, in whatever age of this world's history they might have lived, from Adam to the last generations of mankind. It was a blessing to be enjoyed along with God in the glory of a new life for ever and ever.

b. Previous deliverances achieved for man had only served for some shortlived purpose. Death reigned over all the world, and though there might be a fresh career of glory rising after many a fall, yet the fresh career of glory must perish as that which preceded it. Every renewal of glory had to acknowledge itself subject to the tyrant power. The glory would pass away.

This deliverance was a deliverance from death itself. It would raise from death those who had fallen under its penalty. It would set them free with the security of an endless life. The blessing was Divine. God has sent His Son into the world that all may live through Him, and all who will come unto Him shall henceforth have power to become the sons of God.

c. The manifestation of the sons of God, the restoration of a fallen universe to the glory of the original Divine intention, is not the initiation of a new career of earthly existence which shall after all be exposed to the possibility of failure as the original creation had been. The purpose of God is to be accomplished by the restoration of all things, the restoration of the old organism not in its own weakness but in a mode of existence instinct with the life of the Eternal Son.

All that is not renewed by coming to Him must perish in its corruption. 'A new heaven and a new earth' shall rise out of the grave of sin, glorious with the righteousness of God, and *righteousness is immortal.*

www.ingramcontent.com/pod-product-compliance
Lightning Source LLC
Chambersburg PA
CBHW020806020726
47495CB00008B/2617